HOW TO PLAY LIKE A PRO

BASKETBALL SKILLS

BY TOM ROBINSON

Enslow Elementary

an imprint of

Enslow Publishers, Inc.

40 Industrial Road
Box 398
Berkeley Heights, NJ 07922
USA

http://www.enslow.com

Enslow Elementary, an imprint of Enslow Publishers, Inc.

Enslow Elementary® is a registered trademark of Enslow Publishers, Inc.

Library of Congress Cataloging-in-Publication Data
Robinson, Tom.
  Basketball skills : how to play like a pro / Tom Robinson.
     p. cm. — (How to play like a pro)
  Summary: "Readers will find out how to dribble, pass, shoot, and
defend like their favorite sports stars"—Provided by publisher.
  Includes bibliographical references and index.
  ISBN-13: 978-0-7660-3205-7
  1. Basketball—Juvenile literature. I. Title.
  GV885.1.R624 2008
  796.323—dc22
                                        2007048638
Credits
Editorial Direction: Red Line Editorial, Inc.
Cover & interior design: Becky Daum
Editors: Bob Temple, Dave McMahon
Special thanks to Mike Strong, head women's basketball coach at the University of Scranton, for his
help with this book.

Printed in the United States of America

10 9 8 7 6 5 4 3 2 1

Photo credits: iStockPhoto/U Star PIX, 3, 19, 30, 32, 34, 42; iStockPhoto/iphotomission, 4; AP
photo/Jason Babyak, 7; iStockPhoto/Sergey Kashkin, 8; AP Photo/Jessica Kourkounis, 9;
iStockPhoto/Brandon Beecroft, 10; AP Photo/Matt York, 11; AP Photo/Winslow Townson, 12, 28;
AP Photo/Morry Gash, 13; AP Photo/Darron Cummings, 15; AP Photo/Columbus Dispatch, James
D. DeCamp, 16; AP Photo/Eric Gay, 17; AP Photo/Paul Sancya, 18; AP Photo/David J. Phillip, 20;
AP Photo/Grant Halverson, 21; AP Photo/Frank Franklin II, 22; iStockPhoto/EastWest.Imaging /Phil
Date, 23; AP Photo/Gus Ruelas, 25; AP Photo/Pat Sullivan, 26; AP Photo/El Nuevo Dia, Reinhold
Matay, 27; AP Photo/Phelan M. Ebenhack, 29; AP Photo/Elaine Thompson, 31, 45; AP Photo/Bill
Kostroun, 33; AP Photo/Ross D. Franklin, 35; AP Photo/Matt Slocum, 37; iStockPhoto/Alex Nikada,
38; AP Photo/Tina Fineberg, 39; AP Photo/John Marshall Mantel, 40; AP Photo/Rogelio Solis, 41;
AP Photo/Ed Reinke, 43; iStockPhoto/Bonita Cheshier, 44.

Cover Photo: iStockPhoto/U Star PIX (large image); AP Photo/Elaine Thompson (small image).

CONTENTS

BASKETBALL PREGAME

Basketball players work hard at every practice to improve their skills. Getting that round ball to fall into the basket takes a lot of repetition. Professional players spend hours each day working on their shooting skills.

But basketball is more than just shooting. Dribbling requires great hand-eye coordination, and free-throw shooting is performed best when a player's concentration is at the highest level. Defensive positioning is most effective with players who have an attention to detail. And what player doesn't like to make a perfect pass to assist on a basket?

Basketball is one of the most exciting sports a young person can learn to play. But basketball players are also team players and must be relied upon to be great teammates. More than anything else, the game should be played with sportsmanship and teamwork in mind.

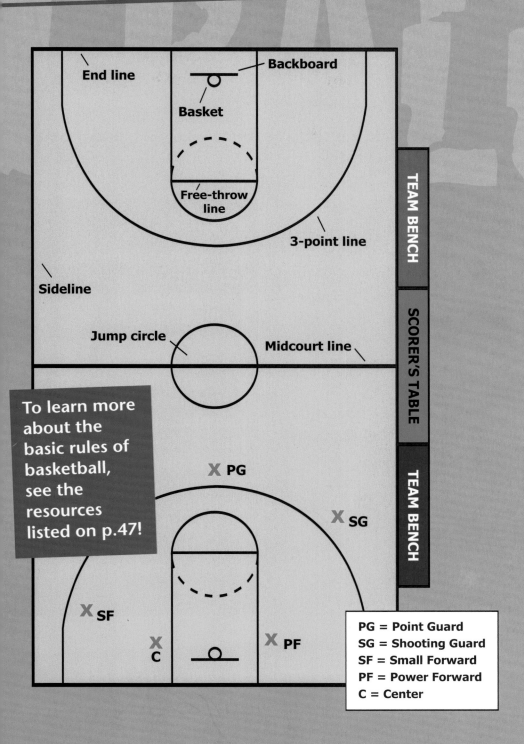

End line

Backboard

Basket

Free-throw line

3-point line

Sideline

Jump circle

Midcourt line

TEAM BENCH

SCORER'S TABLE

TEAM BENCH

To learn more about the basic rules of basketball, see the resources listed on p.47!

X PG

X SG

X SF

X C

X PF

PG = Point Guard
SG = Shooting Guard
SF = Small Forward
PF = Power Forward
C = Center

BALLHANDLING

Ballhandling is one of the most basic skills in basketball. A player who has the ball cannot move around the court unless they are dribbling the ball.

Dribbling is simply bouncing the ball off the floor with one hand. Good dribblers know to use their fingertips, not the palms of their hands, to dribble.

Players may move their feet and change their position as much as they want as long as they are continuously bouncing the ball off the floor.

Practice

Being able to dribble at different speeds and heights allows a ballhandler to move better around other players on the court.

Learn good dribbling technique by standing in one place and getting the feel for the ball. Keep fingers spread and push the ball back to the floor each time. Be sure to use each hand. Notice that when the ball is pushed harder, it bounces back up higher.

A player should not start dribbling until they are ready to move. Dribbling while standing still makes it easy for a defender to stay close.

Double Dribble

Once a player has stopped dribbling by catching the ball—or even briefly putting both hands on the ball at the same time—dribbling cannot be restarted until the ball has been passed to another teammate.

Steve Nash (13) of the Phoenix Suns is one of the best ballhandlers in the NBA. He was named the league's Most Valuable Player in 2005 and 2006.

ADVANCED DRIBBLING

As players get better at dribbling at different heights, they are ready for the more advanced step of changing speeds and direction while dribbling. Players should start by learning to dribble with either hand while running straight ahead at a fast speed. Even while learning to dribble, move with the head up, looking ahead rather than watching the ball.

A crossover dribble is used to switch from one hand to the other. In most straight-ahead or stationary dribbles, the hand is on top of the ball. To cross over, the player moves his or her hand to one side and pushes the ball down at an angle so that it bounces back up to the other hand. In a reverse dribble, a player plants one foot and turns his back to the defender. While spinning around, the player changes dribbling hands.

Practice

Passing the ball through the legs in the form of the number 8 can help a player develop the feel necessary for ballhandling.

Once passing it through the legs is mastered, do the same routine with slow dribbles. Then, try to work up to a faster speed.

Seimone Augustus of the Women's National Basketball Association's Minnesota Lynx (33) uses her dribbling skills to advance past fellow All-Star Sheryl Swoopes (22) of the Houston Comets.

Getting Fancy

Even the most advanced players should limit fancy moves like dribbling behind the back and through the legs to very specific situations. Learning those dribbles, however, can add to overall ballhandling ability.

STOPS & STARTS

Moving the ball from one place to another is a big part of basketball, but stopping and starting can be as important as moving. The proper stops and starts can provide the space necessary for a player to move the basketball effectively.

The player with the ball cannot move more than one full step without dribbling. Therefore, when receiving the ball, a player establishes a pivot foot, planting that foot while moving the other until the dribble is started. By "pivoting" around the foot that is planted on the floor, a player can protect the ball and get into position to try to dribble past an opponent.

Practice

Practice jumping with the ball in your hands, landing on both feet, then pivoting on the left foot. Repeat this by using the right foot to pivot. If a partner is available, jog in a straight line, jump through the air, catch a pass, and land on both feet.

BALLHANDLING

Jump Stop

By using a "jump stop," a player has more options. When catching the ball on the move or in the air, a player lands on both feet, jumping to a stop.

Players can change direction before or after dribbling by pivoting around one foot.

By the Rules

A jump stop at the end of a dribble puts the player in good position to go up in the air for a shot, but does not allow for a chance to pivot and take another step after dribbling.

Tough to Stop

Michael Jordan was such a threat to dribble to the basket that defenders had no choice but to back off. Jordan used that threat to make space for his jump shot.

Using a Screen

If a teammate is in position to screen the defender, the player with the ball should dribble very close to the screener, preventing the defender from getting in between.

A screen can also be used away from the ball to give a player room to receive a pass.

BALLHANDLING

CREATING SPACE

The "jab step" is an effective way of getting space to dribble or shoot.

A player who has just received the ball establishes a pivot foot and steps hard toward the basket or a defender with the other foot. This jab can get the defender to back up and give the ballhandler room to shoot or go a different direction.

Teammates can help create space by setting a "screen," also known as a "pick." The teammate who is setting a screen stands still in a spot that is in the way of where the defender would have to move to guard the ballhandler.

Practice

After receiving a pass from a partner or simply starting from a position similar to receiving a pass, make a quick jab step with the right foot. Bring the foot back and quickly dribble to the left. Repeat, but dribble right. Make the same moves with a left-footed jab step.

As you practice this skill, try to do it faster each time.

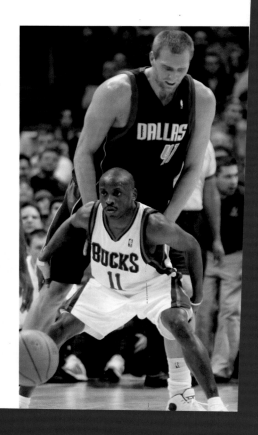

PASSING

The vision of a passer is an important part of the game. If a passer can see a teammate who is open and ready for a shot, there's a chance that the teammate will score a basket. The point guard, or the primary ballhandler on the team, usually generates a lot of assists.

But passing always involves two players, so it is equally important for the pass receiver to see the court well. If the receiver can find an open space, the passer will have a much better chance at making a successful pass.

Passes can vary in distance. Some passes are thrown from one end of the court to the other. At other times, a center with the ball might draw two defenders to cover him or her. In that case, it's easy for the center to find an open player only two or three feet away.

Practice

Dribble with your head up and notice everything to the sides. Use peripheral vision while looking straight ahead to be aware of players as far to the left and right as possible.

An assist is given for a pass that leads directly to a teammate's basket.

Using the Eyes

Eyes are a very important part of passing. Players need to look around the court to see who is open and ready to get the ball. It also helps to look in a different direction briefly to keep the defense guessing.

Tamika Catchings of the Indiana Fever (24) has led her team in assists in each of her first six seasons in the WNBA. She was a gold medalist on the 2004 U.S. women's Olympic basketball team.

CHEST PASS

Fancy passes get attention, but basic passes lead to fewer mistakes and are often more efficient.

The chest pass is thrown with hands balanced on each side of the ball. The thumbs are behind the ball and fingers are on the side.

Look at and step toward the target. Extend the arms and flick the wrists to release the ball with hands pointing in the direction the pass should travel. When the follow through is complete, the thumbs are pointing down.

Practice

Practice stepping toward the target and passing the ball to a teammate's hands without the teammate having to move his or her hands. Practice hitting the target by throwing the ball to a wall or a bounce-back net while concentrating on a specific spot. Try to hit that precise spot.

PASSING

Attacking the Defense

When opponents are in a zone defense, a series of quick passes around the perimeter often opens up space for the offense to attack.

Short Pass

Short passes give the defense less time to react and intercept the pass.

The Target

Chest passes generally are thrown to an open player. Aim the pass at the teammate's chest, allowing the ball to be caught easily, so the receiver can move quickly. When the receiver of a pass has to stretch or reach, more time is needed to be ready for the next pass or dribble.

Step Aside

When a defender is between the passer and receiver, the passer tries to step around the defender to deliver a bounce pass. A bounce pass is more difficult to block than a straight chest pass.

Small But Quick

Some people believe that all basketball players are tall. While many are very tall, smaller players can be good at basketball, too. Being smart and quick are just as important in basketball as being tall.

PASSING

BOUNCE PASS

A bounce pass can be thrown with many of the same techniques as the chest pass. The passer simply aims down at a spot on the floor about two-thirds of the way to the target.

When the passer can step straight at the target, the grip and follow through are the same as a chest pass. At times, it is necessary to step around a defender and lean to one side, however. This naturally puts the hand on that side lower on the ball. Use the lower hand to push the ball forward toward the desired spot on the floor.

The release and target of the bounce pass are lower than the chest pass. It is aimed in the area of the receiver's waist.

Practice

Throw a series of bounce passes to a partner while remaining the same distance apart. Release the ball from different heights and with different amounts of force. Get a feel for how each type of pass gets to the target at a slightly different speed and height.

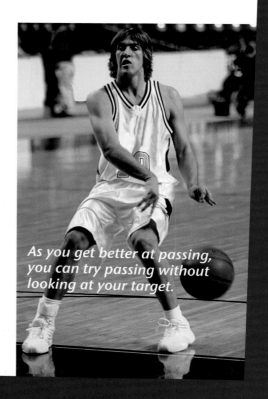

As you get better at passing, you can try passing without looking at your target.

BALL FAKE

Sometimes, it is necessary to trick the opponent to make room to deliver a pass.

Faking up can get a defender to raise his arms, allowing room for a bounce pass. A fake to the left can clear a path for a quick pass to the right.

Make fakes with authority. While keeping a pivot foot, step hard with the other foot and move the ball quickly as if you are making a pass, but stop the motion to hold the ball. The harder and stronger the move looks, the more likely a defender will take the fake and believe the pass is about to be made. Before the defender can recover from the fake, quickly move to the real pass.

Practice

Work on maintaining the pivot foot while stepping in one direction to fake. Then, shift to another direction and release the pass. Step in the direction of the fake target, then in the direction of the actual target while releasing the ball. Also, see how quickly you can raise the ball from your waist to your head.

Mixing It Up

If every pass is thrown with the routine of a ball fake followed by the actual pass, the defender will adjust and anticipate the move.

Instead, mix up the routine. Fake twice before throwing on some occasions and, at other times, make the quick pass before a defender is ready.

It's hard for a player to defend when he is up in the air!

Triple Threat

Fakes are more believable if the defender has to worry about what the player with the ball might do. By starting with the ball in front of the chest, held as it would be for a chest pass, the player is in the "triple threat position" because he or she is ready to shoot, dribble, or pass.

Go to the Ball

Depending on how close the defense is, the receiver should step or lean toward the ball.

When receiving a pass, step or lean in the direction of the pass and always keep your eyes on the ball.

Posting Up

Players who are set up under the basket "post up" to receive the ball. A strong, wide stance makes it more difficult for defenders to get around the receiver and stop a pass.

PASSING

RECEIVING A PASS

In practically every sport, players are reminded to "keep your eyes on the ball." Basketball is no different. Looking each pass into the hands prevents mishandling and dropping the ball.

When being guarded, players must move to get open and in position to receive a pass. When making eye contact with the player who has the ball, a potential receiver can hold a hand high or out to one side. This signals a target and tells the passer where to pass the ball.

Practice

When playing catch, start a little more than fifteen feet apart and have the receiver take one step in while catching a pass. With each pass back and forth, the receiver takes a step in until the players are next to each other.

Move apart again and repeat, switching types of passes from chest to bounce to overhead.

Once you've caught the pass, look for an open teammate.

SHOOTING & SCORING

There are a variety of ways to make a basket.

A player can take an open outside shot, use the dribble to "drive" past opponents, or put the ball in after an offensive rebound.

Being able to use different styles of shots helps make a scorer more effective. Sometimes, a player will have a shot with no defenders nearby. Other times, a defender will reach the shooter and put a hand up just as the shooter releases the shot. Those shots take concentration because the shooter might not be able to see the basket during the release. The best shooters might have two or three defenders surround them to make sure they don't get an open look at the basket.

Count Them Up

Teams receive one point for a foul shot, two for a basket or "field goal," and three for a basket made from beyond the three-point arc. This arc is six meters (nineteen feet, nine inches) from the basket for high school and younger players.

In the NBA, the three-point line is farther away from the basket than for younger players. At its farthest point, the arc is 7.23 meters (twenty-three feet, nine inches) from the basket.

Around the World

When working on shooting, move to different spots, going from one side of the court to the other in an arc similar to the three-point line. Move in a similar curved path to get used to shooting from all angles.

Kobe Bryant led the NBA in scoring for the second straight time by averaging 31.6 points per game in the 2006-07 season.

Bryant has the ability to hit long outside shots and score on drives to the basket. He also draws many fouls and is successful on 83.8 percent of his free throws.

SET SHOT

The set shot—or push shot—is the basis for proper shooting technique in many situations. The shot, which is best for free throws, can be used by an open player.

The set shot also sets the stage for the jump shot by providing many of the fundamentals that are needed to move up to the next level.

Using the legs is important to provide the strength and support necessary to shoot with good form rather than throwing the ball.

The ball is held with the fingertips of both hands. A right-handed shooter puts his or her right hand behind the ball and uses the left hand on the side as a guide.

Practicing good form over and over makes it easier to use it even when distracted in a game.

Practice

When practicing the set shot, start from close range first. Once shots are comfortably going over the rim or bouncing off the target box on the backboard, gradually move back to greater distance.

A strong follow-through completes the proper set shot.

The Release

In one motion as the legs straighten and the hands go up, the ball is released with a flick of the wrists and fingers. The follow-through is complete with the hands held high and the shooting hand waving at the basket after release.

The hand, forearm, elbow, knee, and foot should all be in a straight line.

Always maintain proper balance.

Knees should be bent slightly and feet are apart with the right foot slightly forward. The player crouches a bit more just before starting the shot, then straightens the legs and moves the ball from the chest upward above the head.

Elbow In

Keeping the elbow under the hand helps create the correct release, which leads to the right spin and more shots that roll in off the rim.

Kevin Garnett of the Boston Celtics has averaged more than twenty points per game during his 13-year NBA career.

In a jump shot, the ball is released at the peak of a jump.

HAYWOOD

33

JUMP SHOT

As players progress to higher levels of basketball, developing an effective jump shot is essential.

The jump shot follows many of the same techniques as the set shot, but the player jumps up and releases the ball at the top of his jump.

The increased use of power from the legs creates more shooting range and the higher release makes the shot tougher to block.

Start Low

When learning a new skill, it is important to develop the proper fundamentals.

If you are struggling to reach the basket while learning the jump shot, consider shooting at a lower height while developing the right feel. Once the shot is handled comfortably, begin moving the basket up or switching to a higher basket.

Keep the elbow directly below the shooting hand.

FOUL SHOTS

When players are fouled, such as being bumped, held, hit, or pushed by their opponents, they can get a chance to shoot foul shots, or free throws.

Many games are decided by free throws. Free throws are taken without the defense being able to try to stop the shot.

When a player is fouled while shooting and misses the shot, he or she gets two free throws. If a player is fouled while scoring a basket, the basket counts and one foul shot is awarded.

In addition, each foul in a game is counted toward a team total. If a team commits a certain amount of fouls in a quarter or half, the opponent is awarded "bonus" foul shots. The number needed to reach the bonus is different at various levels of basketball.

Practice

Because the defense cannot try to stop a foul shot, the shooter does not have to worry about being blocked. The best foul shooters usually repeat the same routine every time—such as three dribbles, a deep breath, and a pause before shooting. They usually find a set shot the most effective.

League Leader

Nicole Powell of Sacramento led the WNBA in free-throw shooting percentage in 2007. She made eighty out of eighty-three shots.

Getting Technical

Technical fouls are called for unsportsmanlike conduct. The opposing team is allowed to choose the best foul shooter it has in the game for a free-throw shot before taking possession of the ball.

Lining Up

When a foul shot is taken, players have to stand outside the lane in marked spots on each side. The defensive team gets the closest spots to the basket. The shooting team gets the next spots, and so on.

SCORING

SCORING ON THE INSIDE

The easiest shot in basketball should be a layup. Like any other skill, however, it requires practice.

Dribble at moderate speed toward the basket. On the last dribble, plant the foot closest to the basket, get the ball in both hands and begin to take off into the air. Reach high and release the ball with one hand while getting as close to the basket as possible. Try bouncing the ball off the backboard just inside the top corner of the box that is painted on the board.

Once comfortable, increase speed and shoot layups from both sides.

Practice

The goal for any basketball team should be to get the ball as close to the basket as possible before shooting.

Being closer to the basket, however, does not always mean an easier shot.

Practice by having teammates guard you closely near the basket. Figure out the best way to score. Try shooting, then dribbling and shooting.

Rebounds

Offensive rebounds provide another chance to score. Avoid dribbling and giving players a chance to reach at the ball.

Reach high toward the basket when releasing the ball on a layup.

Pivot

Taller players who play the forward or center position often receive passes close to the basket, but with their backs to the basket. Pivoting on one foot allows for a quick turnaround to a shooting position. The timing of this move requires a lot of practice to do it smoothly.

SCORING IN TRANSITION

Basketball success comes from good offense and defense. The transition from offense to defense or defense to offense is also important.

Teams try to score quickly by running or passing the ball up the floor quickly. This is called a fastbreak.

To run a good fastbreak, the player with the ball moves to the middle of the floor. Other players run up the floor on either side of the ballhandler.

They try to get to the basket quickly, before the defense has a chance to get back and stop them.

Practice

Have a partner stand at the free-throw line. You stand at the end line on the same side of the court. Run past your partner at full speed, and have him or her pass the ball to you when you are at midcourt. Continue to dribble in for a layup. Also try stopping and shooting a jump shot from about twelve feet.

On the Move

The ability to shoot on the move needs to be developed. Remember to plant the foot nearest the basket and push up hard for higher elevation on layups.

Fastbreak

The fastbreak is one of the most exciting plays in basketball. Often, a dribbler goes the length of the floor with the ball. They either make a layup, or they make a quick pass to a teammate for an easy shot.

SCORING

35

DEFENSE

There are two basic defenses in basketball: man-to-man and zone.

In a man-to-man defense, each defensive player is responsible for guarding one offensive player. The defensive player generally stays with the offensive player, making sure to stay between the player and the basket.

In a zone defense, players are responsible for covering an area of the court. They shift within that area depending on where the ball is and the positioning of the offensive players around them.

The importance of playing a strong defensive game cannot be overstated.

Practice

Most fouls in basketball are committed by players who reach in for the ball that is being dribbled or when trying to block shots. Practice jumping straight up and down with hands extended as high as possible above the head. This approach will create a distraction that shooters have to go over.

Jason Kidd's defensive play (at right) helped him become one of the game's greatest guards.

Some of the NBA's best offensive players are also great at defense. Tim Duncan, Kobe Bryant, and Kevin Garnett have all made the NBA All-Defensive team in their careers.

Zones

There are many possible zone defenses. Some teams even use combinations of zone and man-to-man.

The simplest zones are played by many teams.

The 2–3 zone—with two players out in front by the foul line and three along the baseline, protecting the basket—is a common approach to zone defense.

DEFENSIVE POSITION

The proper stance is needed to play well defensively. Proper positioning helps in being able to move quickly from side to side in reaction to an offensive move.

Knees should be bent and feet should be shoulder-width apart. A player needs to be able to get low, especially when guarding a dribbler.

Remember that the offensive player will try to use fakes. Do not watch the ball or the offensive player's eyes or hands. Instead, focus on the player's waist. It is hard for players to make fakes with their waists!

Getting into proper position is essential for good defensive play.

Practice

From a defensive stance, shuffle to the right ten feet and stop. Shuffle back to the left to a spot ten feet beyond the start. Shuffle back to the middle. Avoid crossing your feet over each other as you move. Use short, quick slide steps instead.

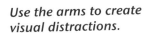

Use the arms to create visual distractions.

Blanket Coverage

Katie Douglas (33) has twice been named to the WNBA's All-Defensive First Team. She was also MVP of the 2006 WNBA All-Star Game.

Knees should be bent and shoulder-width apart.

Players who are away from the ball in a zone defense should keep their hands up or extended from side to side. This keeps the offense from seeing passing lanes and gives the appearance that the players are covering more space than they actually are.

In Transition

When defending in transition, it is best to sprint back into position first. Once back, defenders try to stop the progress of the ball to slow the offense.

While guarding a player, it is important not to lose track of where the ball is.

DEFENSE

DEFENDING PLAYERS

Most of a defensive player's time is spent guarding someone who does not have the ball.

The defender's job is to stay between his or her player and the basket. At the same time, the defender tries to stay between his or her player and the ball.

Practice

Defenders must see the ball and the player they are guarding at the same time. Focus on a spot where you can see both out of the corners of your eyes.

DEFENDING THE BALL

Guarding a player with the ball is an important part of either man-to-man or zone defense.

In a zone defense, once a player has the ball in a defender's area, he or she is guarded under the same concepts used in man-to-man defense.

The defender must be low enough to quickly move from side to side.

Depending on how far the dribbler is from the basket, the defender should give a little space to a dribbler to avoid a drive for a layup. Once the player with the ball stops dribbling, the defender should move closer, making it difficult to pass or shoot.

Practice

Have a partner dribble from side to side using crossovers. Work on shuffling your feet in good defensive position to stay in front of the player. Keep your hands behind your back to eliminate the tendency to reach. Stay low and focus on the dribbler's waist. As you get better at it, have the player dribble faster.

Center of Gravity

Remember to watch a player's waist when defending. While a player may be able to step or reach one way and quickly go the other, he or she can't make a significant move in any direction without moving the center of their body that way.

Defend with the feet instead of the hands, using movement to contain an offensive player. Avoid reaching for the ball unless the dribbler crosses over in a way that makes the ball easy to steal.

REBOUNDING

Rebounding is a two-step process. Players must get into the proper position first. Then they must go get the ball.

When a shot is taken, defensive players turn their backs to the players they are guarding. They attempt to keep the offensive players from getting near the basket. This is called boxing out.

In man-to-man defenses, a player boxes out the opponent he or she is guarding. In a zone, players attempt to box out the nearest player within their zone.

When the ball bounces off the rim, it is important to jump and reach it at the highest possible point above other players.

Practice

Lining up with a part of the backboard to the right or left of the rim, a player can bounce the ball off the backboard and jump to meet the rebound at its highest point. Practice going up to meet the ball and bringing it down with a firm grip. Tip the ball back off the backboard with two hands and jump again.

Outlet Pass

After getting a rebound on defense, a player can start a fastbreak by making an outlet pass. The player pivots away from the basket and looks to the side of the court for an open teammate. This outlet pass begins the transition to offense.

Follow Your Shot

Many missed shots bounce right back in the direction from which they came. The shooter is often the offensive player with the best chance of getting a rebound.

Lauren Jackson (right) is a six-time WNBA All-Star.

GLOSSARY

★ **assist**—A pass that leads to a basket by a teammate.

★ **dribble**—Bouncing the ball repeatedly with one hand to move from one spot to another.

★ **drive**—Dribbling toward the basket.

★ **field goal**—A basket, other than a foul shot.

★ **foul**—An illegal play in which a player hinders an opponent's progress through bumping or otherwise touching.

★ **free throw (foul shot)**—A free shot, worth one point, awarded in some situations after an opponent's foul.

★ **jump shot**—A shot in which the shooter releases the ball at the peak of a jump.

★ **layup**—A shot made close to the basket usually while on the move.

★ **man-to-man defense**—A defense in which each player is responsible for covering one other player.

★ **pivot**—To keep one foot in place while moving the other foot.

★ **rebound**—To retrieve a missed shot.

★ **screen (pick)**—When one offensive player legally gets in the way of a defensive player.

★ **transition**—The switch from offense to defense or defense to offense.

★ **triple threat**—The position from which a player can shoot, pass, or dribble.

★ **zone defense**—A defense in which each player is responsible for a certain area on the court.

LEARN MORE

WEB LINKS

★ **Ducksters Basketball**
http://ducksters.com/sports/basketball.php

★ **NBA.com**
http://www.nba.com

★ **NCAA Kids Club**
http://www.ncaa.org/bbp/basketball_marketing/kids_club/

★ **WNBA.com**
http://www.wnba.com

BOOKS/VIDEOS

★ *Basketball Fundamentals,* by Jon A. Oliver. Champaign, IL: Human Kinetics Publishers, 2003

★ *Basketball Math,* by Jack A. Coffland. Tuczon, AZ: Good Year Books, 2006.

★ *Basketball Steps to Success,* by Hal Wissel. Champaign, IL: Human Kinetics Publishers, 2004.

★ *Rick Pitino-Basketball Fundamentals (video),* Kitchener, ON: Waxworks, Inc., 2007.

INDEX